MY MIND BODY AND SOUL

by SoulSista4Sho

My Mind, Body and Soul

Copyright © 2010 by SoulSista4Sho

All rights reserved. No part of this book may be reproduced or transmitted in any form or by any means without written permission of the author.

ISBN: 978-0-9828242-3-8

Cover Art Design: Bernard 'BJ' Brown, Southern Wave Media

194 Avonshire Drive
Summerville, SC 29483
www.lifechangersenterprise.com

I would like to dedicate this book to the Trinity.
Without Him, NONE of this would be possible.

I would also like to dedicate this book to my heartstrings,
Sincere and Lauryn.

Acknowledgments

To the special man in my life, thank you for your words of love and encouragement, for being by my side through everything.

To my mother, Jannie, who birthed the idea for me to write this book...SURPRISE!

To my children, Sincere and Lauryn, the #1 reason for not giving up and continues to show me love even when they don't understand what's going on with me....SURPRISE!

To my sister, Tia, for connecting me with my publisher when she had no clue what was going on....SURPRISE!

To those who knew about the existence of this project and have prayed and supported me, thank you and I love you with every fiber of my being.

To those who've given me the experiences to write from my heart, I couldn't have done it without you, rather good, bad, or indifferent.

To my publisher, thank you for not giving up on me when I wanted to give up on me! Thank you for your patience and understanding.

Table of Contents

Mind 1

    Gotta Face Reality 2

    Get Away 3

    My Day 5

    To See 7

    Mixed Emotions 9

    Talkin' Loud 11

    How 'Bout Dem Papahs 13

    Confessions 15

    Am I? 17

    The Cycle 18

    Who Are You? 20

    Blame It 22

    Ms. Understood 24

    Solve For X 25

    Manipulation Station 27

    The Sho 28

    Stay Tuned 30

    Stir it Up! 32

    Home 34

    Transition 36

    For A Limited Time 38

    Address 40

    All I Ask 42

    Word on the Street 43

    Boldness 46

    Does Heaven? 47

    Arrival 48

    Front Porch Breezin' 50

    In the Meantime 51

    My Harriett Tubman 52

    Patiently Impatient 54

    Selah 55

Body **57**

    Nakedness 58

    Celebrate Me 59

    Lovin' Me 61

    Soup a la Soul 63

    Initiative 65

    Don't Be Afraid 66

    Mirror Dance 67

Soul **69**

    She Waited 70

    Only You 71

    O.R.D.E.R My Steps 72

    Constant Battlin' 73

    Hell NO!!! 74

    Letter to God... 75

    Too Much! 77

    Dance, Kesha, Dance 79

    Next To Me 80

    No Words, Just Tears 81

The Tested Mother	83
Writer's Block: 3rd Trip	85
The Place	86
The Dwelling Place	87
It's Between Me and You	88
My Expressions of Me (1997)	90

Mind

Gotta Face Reality

As time slowly ticks away
still performing the day to day
tasks as usual
normal so far gone
gotta get used to the "new" norm...
new pants gotta be worn
heart needs to be mended
from being torn
as I make this 180 degree turn
reality is staring me in the face
taking me to a new place
speeding up the pace
on your mark, get set...gotta run this race
to new ventures in life
got reality in my face
like we're head to head
nose to nose...
I guess it is… I suppose…

Get Away

Can I get away like Tupac said?
Lets go somewhere to break bread
communicate, pour my heart out.
Let's roller skate, fall down, "Hey, watch out!"
So much pressure up in here.
Let's just go anywhere
to the park or far away island
walks after dark or just vibin' with the wind.
Get away to the beach right before sunset
to Jamaica in your private jet
or any foreign land.
Walk the coast and bury my toes in the sand.
This all sounds so great and exciting
imagining all of this while in my hoopty riding.
Maybe one day soon
as we gaze up at the stars and watch a full moon
rise for the occasion.
I'm in your arms and we're embracing
and cherishing each moment
like it's the last.
Let's make a toast and raise our glass
taste but don't drink too fast
celebrate the "get away".
Each minute lived, is a minute we won't ever see again.
Let's run for cover because it's starting to rain.

You insist that we just play in the rain
still enjoy'n the getaway.

My Day

My mind often takes me away to sunny days

Beautiful beaches and parks

Long walks after dark

Exchanging beautiful words of love and laughter

Slow love-making after

Songs of intimacy and passion as we dance and embrace

Each other as the melody and words overtake us

It seems like the songs are speaking for us

Everything we've ever wanted to say and do

Every day is fresh and anew and bright

Even when it's not sunny outside

Let's go take a ride anywhere

And stop wondering where the path will take us

The adventure is taking the journey together

Forever with you is what I want

Let's find a spot and lay on the grass

Let me lay on you and hold hands

Reminisce about our past lives and laugh till it hurts

And cry because we're finally freed from it

It's been a long time coming and it wasn't easy

But, since we're together, it's better

Now, let's enjoy this day like it's the last

And sip this wine and watch God's creations

And talk about visiting other nations

Love and security is what I have when I'm with you

My Mind, Body and Soul

As the trees slowly dance with the gentle breeze

We gaze into each other's eyes

And we find ourselves falling deeper and deeper for each other

As the day goes on each second is sweeter than the last

As the sun begins to set each embrace is tighter

Like you don't want to let go

We watch the clouds change colors from white to pink

And then disappears to the other side of our mysterious world

What if we can follow them to the other side

So we can start our day all over again

To See

I want to see
the beauty of Africa
the land...the tan sand
that covers the ground in which ancestors journeyed

I want to see
the strong hills and mountains
that stands against
the open sky

I want to see
exotic animals
unique characteristics
that would make one stand in awe
of the work and wonders that God Himself created
and to contemplate of how Adam thought of each name

I want to see the various tribes
that presently exists
huts, clay pots and art
that the hands of our people created
to see the patterns and colors of clothes
worn by women and children
to see men with their family

My Mind, Body and Soul

I want to see

the faces of my people

to admire the beauty of the people

to hear the variety of dialects and foreign tongues

spoken by my people

I want to sit under a tree quietly

and breathe the air that the ancestors breathed

I want to take a piece of her with me

so that I can have her with me always

~Mother Africa

Mixed Emotions

Mixed emotions got me shook
about an assortment of people, situations,
being content in the midst of heaven and hell-bent bliss,
on the other hand I'm pissed,
on another I wanna be kissed and loved
while gettin' my back rubbed...
get me a glove so I can put this hot situation
on the back burner while dealin' with another of equal value
now you wanna add fuel to the fire by conspiring
WHATEVER it is that don't make a damn bit of sense to me
cause on top of the UNNECESSARY BS I gotta deal wit
You wanna wreak havoc...I got suntin' fo' dat,
gimme a mallet so I can BAM you wit it,
now get SALLY cause now the kids' actin' silly,
lookin' at them side-ways and all willie-nillie!!!
UUUGGGHHH CALGON TAKE ME in a bubble
so I can get away from this trouble
float away to a distant land and maybe listen to a live band
where the breeze can flow with ease through palm trees...
maybe step outta my box
and smoke some weed just for the experience...mixed emotions...
constantly a'mixn' and a'stirrin up the + and −
ingredients of my life's recipes
only to create a well-blended masterpiece
of a real woman that's been chopped and screwed,

whipped by life on maximum speed, kneaded and folded,

now such beauty to behold,

came thru the fire of the oven as pure gold

Talkin' Loud...

Not tryin' to toot my own horn, but TOOT!!!
Lyrical sounds flowing smoothly like a flute
Nowadays I'm trying to make some loot
I know what I am and I know what I'm worth
It seems like I've been doin' this since birth
This comes so natural, no time to rehearse
Compliments are welcomed and appreciated
At times it leaves me exhilarated
At times I become very frustrated
At the words dat people speakin'
Kind words at times
Then others are straight freak and
One day I'mma put ya to the test and
See if you real and what you say will manifest
If you fail, then confess
That you just talkin' to hear ya self speak
All dis jibber jabber
About if you was him
In my face all smilin' and grinnin'
I ain't impressed
With all the mess
That you're sayin'
Portrayin' that you're such a man
And if you had me, yadda yadda, now here comes that plan
Gimme some credit

My Mind, Body and Soul

Thinkin' you go'n get some

Man you'll never get it

I'm wiser than you think

And I ain't actin' like my sh#t don't stink

But I'm at my wits end and on the brink

Of tellin' homies what I really think

Just stop it and let me help you understand

I may not have everything I need

But the strength that I have I'mma proceed

I gotta do what I gotta do

Rather work at Wal-Mart or sell weed

Let's see what the talk's all about

Yappin' and flappin' all LOUD and wrong

Peace out, see ya later, and get the hell on

Be real, stop lyin' and frontin'

Talkin' loud but you ain't saying nuttin'

How 'Bout Dem Papahs

Johnny T said it's cheaper to keep her
I let you back in, kept me and u STILL creepin'
Now alone, you're sleepin'
Still not speakin'...
But it ain't necessary
Cuz dem papahs gah say it all
While you're out there havin' a ball
Receivin' phone calls
From your random chics
Got 'em thinkin' you got it all
You and ya chics 'bout to get ya world rocked
Once you see dem papahs
All you might have left is socks
You may be livin' it up with your absolut and ciroc
Once dem papahs delivered
Your mental is gonna be a toxic shock
I'm researchin' dem papahs as we speak
Don't try to call cause I can't be reached
To negotiate
Or to converse
Cuz homie, it's too late
It's so much that I can take
You thought you can have this cake
And side orders of honey dips
Goin' outta town and takin' trips

My Mind, Body and Soul

Dem papahs say I'mma be stackin' YO chips

Now I'mma be takin' trips and

Takin' sips of ciroc

Celebratin' lovely cuz ya world got ROCKED

Thanks to dem papahs...

(Thanks, Usher!)

Confessions

Put it all on the table

so that we may grow from the issues and

Secrets that's disabled

and stunted the growth of everything that binds

Us together

a relationship that's supposed to last forever

Confessions are professed to free

Us from its strength to control destiny

To lose us from the bind

to control our mind

To become one

no holding back, if so, it wouldn't

Be a flow of freedom

but see um...

If I say it, it may hurt feelings and break hearts

Confessions are the beginning of a new start

Putting faith and words into action

I want all of you,

Not a fraction of you

and if you continue to

Then you don't need me

it's all or nothing baby!

Confessions, confessions, ready or not,

Here it comes!

Maybe not now but definitely later

My Mind, Body and Soul

that tug on your heart

Is gonna become stronger and greater

And pressure is gonna build

so let it out if you will

So that maybe freed from these heavy burdens

The lies, deceits, hurts and manipulations

desired relations

CONFESSIONS, CONFESSIONS!!!!

God just take 'em away!

I've already learned my lessons!

You already know about it so why verbalize 'em???

Take them away because I'm ashamed

there's no one to blame

It was my selfishness and my flesh

That caused these chains to bind

My mind

to be confined

Behind the walls of hurt

the hurt wouldn't

Allow me to open my heart

My heart wouldn't allow you to come in

To come in would allow you to hurt me again

And I don't want to let you in

Something's keepin' me from lettin' you in

But I need God to strengthen me

so that I may begin again...

These are my confessions.

Am I?

Am I supposed to care
When you don't complement my hair?
Am I supposed to allow my heart to bleed
When you make up excuses to leave?
Am I supposed to cry
When you wanna say good-bye?
Am I supposed to wonder why
You continue to lie to me?
Am I supposed to argue with you
Until I turn blue?
Am I supposed to let you continue
To treat me like I'm not 2nd in command?
You want me to fall but I choose to stand
Am I not more than those others
I may be nothing to you, but the bruthas think I'm more...
Am I supposed to allow you to take advantage of me once again?
Never that homie...
This time, it's the end.

The Cycle

Recollecting signs and lies prior affairs
Listening to the constant excuses
Like I'm one of those chics with blonde hair

Am I deaf, blind, or dumb?
Just leave me alone cause I ain't the one
To be messed over
Keep playing and you'll be running for cover
All of this is gonna catch up with you
Sooner than later, I hope
Now, I have to learn how to cope
All over again
Because "The Cycle's" just begun
I'm tryin' to stand still
'Til the battle is over and the victory's won

Patience and longsuffering is something worth having
Wisdom, strength and power is here for the askin'
Can't wait 'til manifestations take place
After this episode has ended
There's no turnin' back
No more re-runs
Or refunds
But, I wish I can at least get my heart back
Now, it's time to get my mind right

Cause I'm about to take flight to embark on a journey

Unlockin' doors that was blocked because now I hold the key

'The Cycle' has ended for me

Who Are You?

WHO ARE YOU???

It amazes me...

That this question arises after a decade + 1 year

In the makin' of a relationship

That sank due to skanks

And drinks that were preferred and consumed

Before what was actually more important

But, it came up short and now...

I'm stumped... (pause)

WHO ARE YOU???

Once again, I ask myself

Which I shouldn't be askin'

Because I should know betta than anyone

But confusion has set in

Portrayal, deceptions, one-sided confessions

Cause you're scared son

That yo' cover will be blown

What's reaped will be sown

Real love was never shown

Actin' all elementary and stupid

But you're a full-grown man

Oh man, the pain

And time wasted on both parties

Just let go so that we may go

Separate ways

AYE MAN, I can't make you stay

I stay silent and pray

While thoughts of anger and violence

I try to keep at bay

But, one day it may sail away and make me stray

WHO ARE YOU???

Still sittin', scratchin' my head

Drownin' in tears as they pour

To the floor

Askin' God "How much more

Do I have to endure?"

Is this the way it's supposed to be?

I doubt that seriously

So bless me so that you can get glory

So bless me, so that someone can love me

The way You desire

Is there anyone I may inquire

Before this life of mine expires?

Blame It

With all of the recent events that has occurred
Somehow, some way I was the blame for it
I was the blame for YOU reaching out to someone else
I was the blame for YOU drinkin' so hard
But I was the one to accept you home
In spite of the mistakes made on both parts,
I thought this was a new start but once again
I've been bamboozled, hoodwinked, lied to, and deceived
I've done most of what I could to be the best wife that I should

I say "most" because the way he was treatin' me,
I couldn't give him my BEST!
Even though I've confessed, that was more fuel for him
To keep doin' what He's been doin'.
It's been a learning process, but I am a product of success
Now, I'm wondering, "What's next?"
I'm waiting for my destiny to Manifest.
I'm trying to keep my head held high,
It's hard ya'll, but I gotta do it for my babies.

Constantly being blamed for nonsense
Blame it on the demons that keep fighting you
Because they see what you have

And don't want you to obtain it

Blame it on the lies that 'they' tell you

Stop blamin' it on me

Ms. Understood

Just because my thought process is different from yours
Just because my mind is open to more things in life
Than constant drama, lies, and strife
I think outside of the box
That you're contained
Don't blame me cause your thought process can't be obtained
Only thinkin' with one side of your brain
Ms. Understood so much, that YOU'RE goin' insane
I admit,
I'm different
It ain't hard to tell
Never claimed to be all innocent
But Ms. Understood is definite
You're nervous now that I'm outta my shell
All the lies you've told is being repelled
Along with the other BS that you like to tell
Ms. Understood – to interpret incorrectly
It's been this way since you've met me
If you wanted to understand,
You would've made it a necessity
But on the contrary
I remained
MS. UNDERSTOOD

Solve For X

GOOD MORNING SUNSHINE!!!

Another chance for my mind to unwind

And release yesterday's issues

And throw out the wet tissues

From the tears

As I reflected back on the years and times of old

Memories and dreams yet to unfold

I plan to have a great day

No matter what comes my way

Determination, strength and a high self-esteem

Is what I need

I'm glad that I have people in my corner that pray and intercede

On my behalf

Because what I'm goin' through is like bad math

Nothing is adding up

But I continue to add and you keep takin' away

By subtracting the little that I have

Then want to carry over to the next problem

Which causes me to divide and conquer

Which isn't right

When we're supposed to be fruitful and multiply

But I guess we gotta weigh it out

We have more pluses than minuses

But it's only a fraction of what I deserve

I don't believe that you have the nerve

My Mind, Body and Soul

To think that I don't have what it takes

But the problems keeps compiling

And they expect me to keep on smiling

Like nothing's wrong

I'mma keep writing rhymes

And keep singing songs

Because this problem can't be prolonged

We gotta find the square root

Of the cause and effect

And solve fo X

Manipulation Station

Next stop, MANIPULATION STATION...
Once again, the saga continues
On goes the lies...yadda yadda
You want some cheese to go with that wine
Don't use current affairs
For hidden agenda and the unawares
Don't use tragic events
To develop false contentment
No time for extra resentment
This current situation
Only brings more frustration
This only pushes me further away
And wishin' that I can move TODAY
Can't wait for the day to come
Can't be happy with me
So you just lost one

The Sho

LIGHTS, CAMERA ACTION
No time for integers and fractions
Don't want nada mucho from you
I want the whole enchilada

The SHO must go on regardless of the situation,
Oh, did I forget to mention
that it has NOTHING to do with you, I'm doin' this for me
it's time to face reality that maybe we'll never be
for the simple fact that obviously
it didn't work the very first time...lie after lie, for quite some time
I knew that you won't always be mine
but I'll be fine with the outcome of this situation,
freedom, peace, and lots of passion
is what I'm lookin' forward to cause it's LONG overdue

The SHO MUST GO ON cause freedom is my focus,
knowledge to know this, battle ain't mine in da first place,
you took my heart and erased it to make careless but never-the-less

THE SHO is gonna proceed, yes indeed,
it started kinda slow but I gotta speed up the process
and move on to what's next,
preparing for the next episode to be present on CHANNEL LIVE,
to show what's been deprived but this time I'm on the rise

to new horizons and plateaus, lights, camera, action,

to keep you in the know, now STOP and POSE,

look directly at my nose

cause this photo will be posted as a warning for the next few ho's

who thought they knew who you were

cause the SHO preferred to not to settle

VVVVRRROOOOOOMMMMM movin' fast

cause I had to press the gas pedal

cause THE SHO MUST GO ON!!!

Stay Tuned

Stay tuned to channel "Soul"
for up-to-the-minute
love, joy, pain, and insanely comical
freestyles and word play that I haven't done in a while

Stay tuned
for the latest relational drama
hurtful karma
periods, question marks and commas
that separate lyrical phrases
of life's cycles and stages

Stay tuned
for the self-encouragement
that I have to tell myself on the daily
being hopeful that maybe
one day
that special someone will tell me voluntarily
about the beauty and grace that he appreciates
in a woman of such "SOUL"

Stay tuned
for the variety of feelings
that's bursting through the seams
of my heart that's bound to be heard

from this to that and the third

Stay tuned

to lyrical genius

entitled "Chocolate Legs" to "Just Words, No Meaning"

Coming to a stage near you...

My Mind, Body and Soul

Stir it Up!

Gifts and talents lie dormant
as they await the seed
that'll bring life
and bring forth strength in a such a way
that's powerful enough to rock and knock the
whole word off its axis
As the seed starts its aquatic
journey to nurture these gifts and talents
that's about to come forth
I can feel each stroke of motion
waves of emotions
high and low tides of life that dances with the moon
It's like He's got a majestic spoon
stirring up the gifts in me
I can't keep still
I'm restless
like there's a-mixin and a-stirrin'
goin on in my belly
Here comes words of encouragement
psalms of love and passion
phrases of laughter and comedy
silly enough to scratch ya head in wonder and amazement
only to ask "Why did it take so long for this awesome-ness to take place?"
The answer is: all the ingredients that it takes to make this lyrical con-

coction wasn't available:

a dab of creativity

a lil of originality

a tad of growth

a smidgen of humility...now stirred all together

and you got

SoulSista4Sho!

Home

Yesterday began my transition to a new place called home.
As I hung each picture and curtain
I was more certain that this was the right thing to do,
very much long overdue
as the sun played peek-a-boo with the clouds
being here made me proud.
The sun finally made the awaited appearance
and made it known
as it shown
thru my windows and warmed my heart as it filled my home.

A queen of my own throne,
a place of peace and serenity
filled to the brim and overflowing to my surroundings
a place of solace and escape
HOME!

Reminiscin' about the good and bad
which is what made ME the woman I am
God bless my Home,
so that I may find rest
and continue my quest for more
there's more in store for my life
no time for gripes and complainin' n this place called
HOME!

A breath of fresh air filled my lungs
and exhaled with satisfaction
No more settling for fractions cause

now I'm whole in my HOME.
God bless the child who got his own...HOME.

Transition

This transition puts me in a position
to uproot my children
from a false sense of comfort known as home.
So many thoughts goin' through my dome.

I must stay focused cause I'm on a mission—
in spite the situation and status.
I wanna go as high as a cloud maybe a stratus...

Actions speak louder than words
character assassinations may occur
because I got the nerve to make a life changing decision
because my mind is precisely tuned to what he's tryin' 2 do 2 me
think he got me in his hands like silly putty.
Certain things he did drove me nutty
Now, I'm like quit buggin' me!

I can see clearer now on my knees
and takin' a bow to the ONE
and his begotten Son
for protection and faith and strength that I've made it THIS far
in a car that's barely runnin' with a lil prayer and anointing oil
just tell me where and I'll be there being happy and spoiled
even though it needs a heating coil

Just throw on some extra layers and a blanket to improvise
'til it gets better;
keep my eyes on the prize – it's only temporary
but this transition is SO NECESSARY.

For A Limited Time

Why is it that some bruthas sho a lil' interest

and let it be known

and you give a lil back...

and then they forget about you

until anotha' brutha sho just a lil bit mo'???

and NOW you got issues

because you didn't pursue as hard as you should,

so, now you're questionin' about the "other dude".

I'm available for a limited time only

don't expect me to wait around until you make time for me

life is short and my life is mine

maybe I'll see you next lifetime like Sista Badu suggests.

So, don't walk around like "Oh, I got you,"

thinkin' I'mma be by your side like Sade Adu

but you keep thinkin' that time is on your side.

I'mma pass you by like that girl did the Pharcyde

if you really wanted me you would've done

what's necessary but oh well,

you lost cause I'm available for a limited time only.

Address

For some time I figured that if I address certain situations
It may bring closure.
Exposure may make it go away
If I address it, will it stay away?
Stay gone?
Not to be reborn?
Not to revisit?
STAY DEAD!!
Stay buried in my past life
Stay away, 'cause I got a knife!
I'm armed and dangerous!
And I've had enough of this stuff
Repetitious mistakes, hurts, pains, and the such
Hell, ya'll know where I've been,
You know, my experience
A lot has happened since I've been away
And I ain't going back there
Never, never no more
I have no more energy to address this mess, the same stresses
I'm on to new things
New levels, new devils, they say.
But I got something for that too
I may drink a glass or two to mellow out
'cause at times I wanna scream and shout,
Cry and/or pout

But it's alright, it's only temporary

I'm not gonna address it

I'm not gonna suppress it either

I'm gonna express it on my knees

And ask the Father to please

Give me peace

Take away the disease

Make me feel at ease

Heal me, mold me, and console me

Renew me—mind, body, and soul

Take control

Father address the hurt, the pain,

Keep me from losing my brain

Even though at times I wanna hop a train

Or take a flight on a plane

Just to get away and maybe STAY away…

To a new address

All I Ask

All I ask is that you listen to my heart

Laugh with me, cry with me, honor me and respect me

Don't judge my mistakes or short-comings

Walk with me and be glad to be with me

Be silly with me and dance with me

Look into my eyes and pull me close to you

Feel my pain and my pleasure!

Hold my hand as we travel thru this land called life

Let's experience togetherness forever

Allow me to love you the way you need and desire

Don't be afraid to let go,

Don't be afraid to let me

Don't be afraid to have me

'cause I'm not afraid to let go

Word on the Street

Surprisingly some information

Has been in circulation for quite some time

I pick up the phone

and now it's on!

Confirmed but very personal details

Has been piercing the ears

Of those nosey ones or maybe people who just don't care

About what's real

All they do is just cop-a-squat and say "YO, WHAT'S DA DEAL???"

Word on Da Street is just what it is to most

But when it comes to me and mine,

I wanna make an approach

But I gotta lay low

So the sources won't know

that I know and what they know, I can 4 SHO

Use it to represent my case

Gotta keep it tight...no time to waste

Word on Da Street normally travels fast

and will come back like a boomerang

and hopefully not to kick you're a$$

when the real word on da street

decides to mysteriously take leak

this time...they'll be the one playin' hide-n-seek

no need to run, no need hide

You'll be the one lookin' for a place to reside

At Least He...

"At least he comes home to me..."

What does that supposed to mean?
Does that mean that he does whatever he wants while you're hoping things will get better?

"At least he comes home to me..."

Does that means he can sleep around and bring home various STDs?

"At least he comes home to me..."

Sounds like a phrase of desperation!
She can do better than THIS!!!
Look in the mirror!
Look at your God-given beauty and talents!
After days and nights of worry and frustration--Calgon take me away!
She doesn't care if it's all that way to Rome!
Just to get away from it all, while he's out there havin' a ball!
People look and wonder what's wrong, like you've aged 10 years and you're only 27!!!

"At least he comes home to me..."

What a shame that foremothers and women used to say this...
she called mama, friends and church sisters for encouragement
as a result they're asking her questions from adultery to physical abuse.
Lips slightly open to say no but it hurts just as bad as if he did hit her!

"At least he comes home to me..."

How can she settle for less?
She's supposed to have God's best
even though circumstances puts our faith into TEST mode
just to see how long we can hold
to HIS unchanging hands.
Sitting quiet and still 'cause we don't know His master plan.
She wanna rise up and take a stand.

She must remain on her face and knees
while asking God for strength and peace
and protection from whatever disease he may expose her to.

"At least he comes home to me…"

…was the last time she said those words.
While all hell broke loose,
God made ways that no man could change.
He arranged while drama happened
things she had no control of but later on fitted like a glove.

"At least he comes home to me…"

…was no longer in her daily dialogues.
She thought her conversations with God were a monologue.
She didn't hear HIS voice 'cause she didn't know HIS voice.
She trusted Him 'cause she had no other choice!
'Cause of her obedience and faithfulness,
He blessed her with the best!

She's walking tall, head held high,
self-confidence increased with every stride,
no longer looking aged and saddened...
rejoice like nothing ever happened!
She doesn't have to say that phrase anymore
'cause she has a man that's proud to come home to her!!!

Boldness

You've allowed your boldness
To unfold a mystery to my unknown
Revelation led me to the unsolved
Mystery that helped me make a lifetime decision
Quite obvious you're more than friends
But all the while pretended
That's all you've been
You've claimed there were more to follow
Frustrated, irritated…
I tried not to allow hate to infiltrate my heart
Because that wouldn't be so great
I don't wanna be bitter and angry because of the deceit
Constantly repeating itself like a broken record.
This time I've learned a hard lesson from life
Painful as it may seem, the anesthesia taken kinda numb the pain from the knife that's been stabbed in my gut
But I chose to move forward, face reality and be free

Does Heaven...?

Does Heaven have BMX bikes
with dirt roads where we can ride all day and pop wheelies?

Does heaven have trees with pink fuzzy flowers you can climb
and hang upside down from?

Does heaven have basketball courts and a kickball field?

Does heaven have ditches so we can catch tadpoles and play 'dead man'?

Does heaven have glass containers and different pots so we can play 'poo-kum-pot' to fill them with different sands, dirt, rocks and grasses?

We played outside for hours at a time!

Does Heaven have that special tree we once sat under and had a talk about "life" at our young ages?

I hope Heaven has all the things we've experienced because Earth is pretty lonely without you!

I'm missing you, Jr.

Arrival

Some time ago I've embarked
on a journey of an assortment of emotions
like a bag of skittles
heart was brittle
now damn near broken
Always wishing, praying and hoping
for more
always looking forward for what's in store.
On the road of my life
has a lot of one way streets,
Dangerous curves and detours
Of wanting to explore
The what-ifs
and how-comes
was careful not to run
off the road
so let me back up and get back on course
more rocky bumps on this journey
unknown of the destination
on this daily journey
one day at a time
one step at a time
on the way there were words
released
with or without meaning

some encourage, some are unseeingly

surprised that most were discouraging

actions were excused silently

which made me to react violently

but I must continue with the silent treatment

often times days and weeks went by

with heart-hurting sighs

But I gotta stay on my path

not too far to go

gotta by-pass

negative stress and triumph over these obstacles

In order to get to my arrival.

Front Porch Breezin'

Enjoying God's creation
as I watch nature happen
before my very eyes, as I sit on the front porch breezing;
allowing my mind to ease
I'm at peace
While I enjoy the breeze.
As I sit on the balcony,
Sweet memories come back to me
Reminiscing about my life as a child
In the yard running wild
With cousins and siblings
Playing made up games as children
Front porch breezin'
It's such a relief to breath in
and out the fresh air
Up at the sky, I stare in amazement of the wonders of my God.
I find it odd
As to why people don't take the time and enjoy front porch breezing
Kick back and relax, fill the air with laughter
Especially after a long day's work
And people irked your nerves
We all deserve a moment of peace and serenity to regain sanity while
front porch breezin'

In the Meantime

Trouble on every hand
Don't know which way to turn
We pray and cry and wait and wait some more

In the meantime…
We stand still because there's nothing else to do
Allow God's blessings to manifest in our lives
Praise and worship God for what He's already done
And what He's about to do

In the meantime…
Look back at where He's brought you from to where you are now

In the meantime…
Take a walk on the a beach
Or in a park and admire God's beauty and creation
The awesome wonder and mysteries

In the meantime…
Adore Him for how he made you
Look in the mirror and just look at how
God made you and your uniqueness and admire
How special and different you are

In the meantime….
Take time to breathe
Allow Him to let go of the hurt
And the pain and the struggles of life

My Harriett Tubman

When I need a place of protection from the bullshit,
when I wanna place just to talk and sit,
when I need a prayer,
When I need to hear
from the Lord
or just to go over if I'm bored
A place of refuge is what I call it.

A woman of grace and strength and great faith,
A woman that doesn't mind sharing her space
with anyone that she can help.
Words of encouragement are more than heartfelt.
She has also dealt with the hand she has been dealt...
She is my Harriett Tubman!

She has been there when I needed to be lead to freedom.
She has been my protector in the middle of the night.
She has been there to stop possible domestic fights.
But see um,
She's a warrior
and she's always there for ya!
Only to be lead by the Holy Spirit
humorous and quick-witted

My Harriett Tubman...

You would think we are as close as cousins.
She raised five kids with no husband...
she had struggles of her own
and always on the phone.
Being a listener
is what she does best;
working her business
with little to no rest
AND STILL dealin' with her personal stress!
When it is time to go, she knows how to dress
for the occasion.
She is a natural healer
like Aloe Vera to an abrasion
MY Harriett Tubman is who she is

Patiently Impatient

I have been waiting anxiously for this mysterious lover,
a lover that my heart so desires
I'm in dying need of a companion
that I can hold hands with as we walk sandy beaches
I'll listen as he teaches me the unknown.
As the phones go unanswered,
we also dance and prance to enchanted music,
eat fruit along with alcoholic fluid
That gets us loosed but not too loose
Just enough to be infused
I've been impatiently waiting time spent
with the one whose heaven sent
Just groovin' and getting' down in the sunshine,
as I feel him caress my spine with such a gentle touch
ooohhh, it doesn't take much to turn me on to him
I get a shiver just to see him grin
Patient impatience often get me frustrated
with waiting but I have no choice
Impatience almost seems like negligence
my heart is filled with the desire
to voice the pain that I feel
when potentials just wanna play games
and take my for granted,
so now I feel slighted and slanted
but blessed because access hasn't been granted
to allow the hurt to beyond a flesh wound
still hoping that my king will soon come
Patient impatience henceforth I will wait for him
to arise as the sun on a crisp morning
Maybe God is still forming him especially for me
But I'll wait patiently

Selah *(Pause and think calmly of that)*

Situations may seem out of control for the moment
I have to remember that situations are temporary
Selah…
I must remain calm
Remember there is a balm
That heals all hurts and wounds
Remember that the morning will soon come
Selah…

Situations may seem out of control for the moment
I have to remember that situations are temporary
Selah…
Just be and be still
Remember His will
Know that trouble won't last always
Cherish your days
As it comes
Selah…

Situations may seem out of control for the moment
I have to remember that people are necessary
Selah…
Enjoy the people encircled
Laugh 'til you turn purple
Love today
Love always

Body

Nakedness

As I lay here in my nakedness
with nothing on but my blackness
enjoying each breath
as the worry and stress exits
I'm basking in my nakedness
open with nothing to hide
uncovered with pure beauty
that I behold
pure as gold, with nothing but treasures to be unfold
my nakedness
softly caressed, thoughts of love takes flight
desiring that one to spend my days and nights
with...wishing my imaginations were reality
layin' with you and just being free
enjoying every moment from start to finish
beholdin' our nakedness

Celebrate Me

I'm that woman that's worth celebrating
From my natural licorice locs
To my skittle toes and pedicure feet
And my chocolate chip freckles that's sprinkled all over my body
Not your "average-sized" woman though
I got these sweet cinnamon rolls but it's all good!!!
I'm that woman you wanna sink your teeth in
Make you wanna ask, "Where the hell you been?"

Celebrate me because I'm worth it!
I love to laugh, I love life,
I love sunny days and satin nights
I love to cook and clean
And anything in between
I love long bubble baths
And drenching in scented oils
Carol's Daughter got me spoiled

Celebrate my spirit-filled mind
Celebrate my thick behind
Celebrate me because I'm not your average woman
I got a mind of my own and I am strong
I'm willing to do what it takes to make it
Celebrate me because I'm unique
Celebrate me because I can be your lady

My Mind, Body and Soul

As well as your freak
Celebrate me because I'm from the country
Country cooking, country grammar
That good ole' country flava!

Celebrate me because I'm a child of the King
and that's the reason why I sing
Celebrate me because I'm me
I ain't tryin' to be like no other
Can't be duplicated, never overrated
And never underestimate my strength,
My power and the possibilities are endless
When I'm not feeling my best
Cause I'm that woman that you don't wanna test

Celebrate me because I celebrate me!
I dance, I prance
I sing and I can bring it
And I can swing my hips to that song with a slammin' beat
From the horns to the high hat
Celebrate me because I'm all that!

Lovin' Me

I love me so much

each touch so magical

The way my two-toned locs gently flows to the back of my neck

The way my skin glistens after a soothing shower

the way it glows after the application of baby oil

as it gently runs down

curves so round and voluptuous

the softness along with firmness

of my sweet cinnamon rolls

rubbin' in and hoping not to miss any spots

not your average-size brown beauty

while lookin' at my eyes, deep brown and sensuous

to look into them will have you delirious

each chocolate-chip is placed ever so perfectly

in places never imagined

I love me so much

that I have to make sure every fiber

of my body is as close to perfection

as possible for me and maybe HE will know

how to be ever so careful because I only have one

Each toe dazzle with glitter and glitz

lips still glossin' after a lil sip

Lovin' me so much...

my fingertips admire parts that went untouched

the thought of love-makin'

My Mind, Body and Soul

instantly awakens

Ms. Chocolate Cherry, got sweet juices overflowin'

wishin' that there was one with a special bowl

not to miss a drop of sweetness

but I'm lovin' me so much

that I could care less

cause the way I'm feelin' right NOWWWW, ooooooo Baby

ain't no if's, and's or maybe's

cause this feelin right'cha

got me a lil crazy and besides myself,

but oh well, I'm lovin me

Soup a la Soul

Warmish-hot water fills my bowl
of degradation careful not to let it overflow
along with gentle scents of lavender and chamomile
candles carefully lit
its lights creates an atmosphere of peace and tranquility
instrumentals of acoustic guitars and horns
breaks the silence
a quick feel of the water to make sure the
temperature is safe to enter
the ingredients for SOUP a la SOUL.
First enters feet
then the rest sure to follow
mmmmm...this feels good
my body is immersed
covering all of God's brilliance
and beauty of a mass of flesh
a long sigh of breath released
thru semi-glossed lips
a bead of sweat slowly drip
as I begin to take a sip of wine
to ease my anxious mind
cinnamon locs dampened just a tad
but oh man, it ain't enough to get mad
soakin' away all of the day's stress
not allowing worries to manifest.

SOUP a la SOUL

an array of shades of brown

a face of a slight frown

dissolved into a smile

reminiscin' about some real good times,

potential rhymes and

get a bowl and come get some!!!

Initiative

Let me know that you miss being in my presence

Pull me close to you and see what happens next

"I miss U 2 baby!"...in my lil sexy voice

I have no other choice

But to reciprocate the favor

Oh baby, we're too loud, let's not awaken the neighbors

With all this love we're makin'

We didn't even make it to the bedroom

Through the door and in less than 60 seconds, I'm naked

Now, that's what I call taking the INIATIVE

And being spontaneous

Keep doin' it! No one will be able to come between us

Cause every time I see you, feels like I wanna bust

Without one touch...INIATIVE.

Don't Be Afraid

Time together is precious

I can never get enough of YOU

I gave you something that you aren't aware of

That something that I gave is my heart

And I wasn't afraid

because I saw yours

I look deep into your soul

and I listen to the compassion in your voice

I feel every emotion and vibe

please don't be afraid

I know pain all too well to hurt another

I know how it feels

I know how NOT to hurt others

I need you too much to be afraid

I desire and crave you

I want you too much

We're takin' this journey together

hand in hand, side by side

day by day

so please don't be afraid!

Mirror Dance

Before steppin' into the shower
I had to take a glimpse of all this brown power
a quick glimpse took nearly an hour
admiring God's creativeness
from locs to breasts
down to mid-section
O LORD, what a blessing
to have all ah dis and
loving every fiber of my being
not trying to be conceited
just loving me from head to feet
and everywhere in between
strike a pose...looking up to the sky
towel dangles between my thighs
got my own rhythm playing in my head
from side to side goes dreads
doing my 2-step
as I do my mirror dance
looking behind me as I uh, uh, uh, and prance
God's awesome beauty
no need for enhancements
just a lil gold eye shadow and lip gloss
leaving you enchanted
telling myself...

"GO BIG GIRL and DO DAT MIRROR DANCE"

Soul

She Waited

I have never met anyone so passionate about wanting and loving a husband

Wanting to make him feel like a special man

to share and to cherish special memories 'til the end

Friends came and left

and she was left with a broken heart

Broken in the same place as the last

It took some extra healing and mending as only One could perform

She did not stop there because she knew that she had to go on

Prophecy after prophecy has been told and she knew it would happen

She pondered and prayed and she waited

Then, her special love manifested

Now she has been blessed with such a man!

Now blessings and love is overflowing

Why?

Because she waited

Only You

Only You know how my life has been
From childhood to adulthood
Twisted and toiled like a whirlwind

> Only you can heal years of pain
> And give me strength to regain
> Everything that's been lost

Only you can reach down into my soul
Only you can give me heart as pure as gold

> Only you know my end from my beginning
> Only you loves me even when I'm sinning

Only you can renew my mind from the past
And keep me from pressin' rewind

> Only you see me when no one else does
> and give me peace like a dove

Only you know my heart's desires
And what sets my soul on fire

> Only you can give me the strength when I wanna let go
> Only you can hold me and tell me no,
> My child just hold on a lil while longer
> These trials are only to make you stronger

O.R.D.E.R My Steps

O-OBTAINING
R-REVERENCE for
D-DIRECTION
E-EDIFICATION
R-RESTORATION/REFRESHING

O.R.D.E.R. my steps so that I may walk in your will
Help me to listen and teach me how to be still
And know that You are God

O.R.D.E.R. my steps so that I may stand corrected
At times I feel disconnected
Because of the current distractions and hindrances
I don't want my past actions
To take me backwards

O.R.D.E.R. my steps so that I may stay grounded
Because I don't wanna to ever become too high
So that I can't look up to You
Help me to stay surrounded
By positive people
Who sees me as their equal
This life's journey now has a sequel
To the last episode
Keep me grounded so that I won't explode

O.R.D.E.R. my steps to keep me sane
I don't wanna develop an overload of the brain
Keep me in O.R.D.E.R.
So that I won't have a disorder
No situation is worth lettin' myself go
I gotta be here to watch my seeds grow

Constant Battlin'

My soul's cryin'
Like I'm dyin'
Stop denyin' the sin that was so satisfyin'
But I had to stop sinnin'
Cause Hell wasn't gonna win for an instant ten
Gotta repent daily
So daily I gotta go back to the gate
Daily I gotta say I'm sorry
This evil won't stop botherin' me
Obviously...
It's a constant battle
Stay strong...but also feelin' fragile and weak
Eat some apples
Or drink some green tea Snapple
I gotta win
I can't pretend any longer
Each day I'm strong, weak, and then stronger
Gotta play some worship song
Lord keep me near the cross
Praising my Savior all the day long
Battlin' is what I call it
Surrender or forfeit
But I can't forget
The battle ain't mine anyway
Gotta stay on my face
Thankin' Him for grace and
Mercy...for constantly keepin' me!

Hell NO!!!

There were many times that I've allowed adversity to take a place in my life and I didn't know how to handle it.
I would pray but there was a lil doubt present.
I didn't use the authority that I've been blessed with
and once upon a time, I didn't know that I possessed it.
So now, I have a different approach
whenever adversity presents itself
I stare it in the face and say "HELL NO!"
Because did not give us the spirit of fear; he gave us authority!

HELL NO, you're not gonna steal my joy!
HELL NO, you're not gonna keep my family in bondage!
HELL NO to financial disparities!
HELL NO to sickness and pain!
HELL NO to the world's way of life!
HELL NO to generational curses!

I'm taking a stand for my life and the life of others in my circle
even if that means screaming HELL NO 'til I turn purple!
I'mma have a boldness like Steve Urkel,
He was wimpy didn't take NO for an answer.
I hope this message spread like cancer.
And once it's heard I'mma take a bow like a dancer

Letter to God...

I am ANGRY!

I won't allow this emotion to get the best of me

Strengthen me

Please heal me

I've allowed my vulnerability

to make me such a fool

Mistakes were conceived from stupidity

This turned me

into a person that I'm not proud of

Ashamed of

That's not me in my entirety

Mistakes could've taken my life away

You've given me grace

I was such a fool to react because of revenge

The thought of it makes me cringe

I want to begin again and again and again

The words you've said to the woman at the well,

"Go and sin no more"

Please heal me and take away the guiltiness

And the fights with myself

The sleepless nights by myself with no one to hold

I find comfort and safety in your presence

I've been such a fool, such a fool, God!

Make it go away

The bitterness,

My Mind, Body and Soul

the anguish,

the selfishness

its only there because I've been

burned by many issues

and the walls have been built that's hard to tear down

many days I've worn a frown

I can't continue to let this keep me down

Things are going well and I just can't give up now

So, continue to mold me

Shape me, control me

Bless me and uplift me

So I can be me, freely…

I'm tired of being angry

Too Much!

Too much on my mind

I need an outlet

I need to vent

Mind bogged down with heaviness

Stress from issues with children, a silly ex-husband

My health, my wealth

Trying to figure out what's best

I need two weeks' vacation just to rest

I'm up to my breast with frustration

I need some verbal or mental elation

At this point relations with vaginal penetration

Won't be enough

I need a hug…

To be held tightly until I'm freed from this nightmare

Too much on my mind

Trying to do so much

To stay on my grind

Time is so short

All sorts of ideas, thoughts

Both negative and positive

Live in my mind

Fear of losing love

Fear of not having enough

Tired of people calling my bluff

My Mind, Body and Soul

Tests and trials

Constant denials and doubt

Always cloud my mind

Thinking "this could be a sign"

Tired of the rigmarole

The back and forth

Going to and fro

With either or neither

Here or there

I just wanna get outta here!

Lord free my mind

Seems like I don't have time for anything else

In desperate need of great peace

To overtake me

A great sense of serenity to endow me

Bestow me with freedom

So that my mind can be at ease

~~fin

Dance, Kesha, Dance

Dance, Kesha, dance

Show your stuff and prance

In the Spirit!

Hands swaying in the air

doing your dance like you just don't care!

As you twistin' and a' twirlin gets us lifted

A beautiful, young lady so gifted!

Allow your arabesques to move the crowd,

to usher us in to his presence

so we may rest in His bosom

Always allow him to use you anyway and anyhow

Dance tall and dance with pride

One day, you'll make a beautiful bride!

When I see you dance, tears well up inside me

you break down walls and barriers so that we can be free!

So, dance, Kesha, dance

Take a twirl and jump up and prance

we will all stand as you take your bow!

Next To Me

Next to me, I watch you sleep

So precious and peaceful

Skin deep chocolate, soft and sweet

I wanna caress you as I watch you sleep

But I dare not disturb you

I wanna kiss your face as I watch you.

I wanna make love to you so slow and passionately

So slow and delicately.

I wanna kiss your eyes

As I listen to you breathe.

To see you sleep after our love session, you're in a place of peace

We've created a memory that can never be deleted

Next to me you lay

I wanna wake you

because these feelings of love are once again trying to overtake me

Next to me, I'm trying to control

These feelings I behold

No Words, Just Tears

Heart heavy

Like the weight of the world is on it

Hanging by a string

My brain can't comprehend

What my heart is trying to form

Moans and groans is all that is understood

Closed doors,

Windows of opportunities sealed shut by Gorilla glue

Complicated people everywhere

Trying not to develop hate for

My quiet storm has become a violent hurricane!

The pain so strong that even Novocain can't soothe

I refuse to allow pain to make me insane

Tears roll down my window pane

Tears for various reasons

Tears in and out of season

At times words can't be formed

Most times words has no explanation

Tears roll down as they bring relief

To my heart burns

As my world continues to turn and hold on to its axis,

I ask Jesus to help me

These three words come with the tears most of the time

More words form without a scheme or a rhyme

Just tears, just tears, just tears

The Tested Mother

Twin babies were expected earlier than the date received
After birth she had to leave them overnights about an hour away
Which is too far away
Day by day for months and months she made her way to the facility
to nurse and nurture these babies,
so precious and little but so strong and curious
The blessings that were given
are now taken away because of negligence and ignorance
something that happened over 8 years ago.
Days and nights spent crying and praying
while her children are laying in different homes
as she sat at home or slavin' at work
or gaining an education and knowledge at school or wherever!
She didn't stop, not one time did she stop!
She didn't give up, in spite of what the people said,
no matter what lies he said or the games they played;
she continued to lay at His feet
defeating the enemy of her soul
as government facilities try to take control of her life!
Go here, go there, take this, do this, do that:
she's done EVERYTHING that was asked and demanded,
fake friends came n left, trying to be all sweet n candid
and they STILL didn't satisfy her desire to fill those empty voids.
I'm sure she became annoyed n frustrated
that she did everything and demonstrated

that she's a great mother but to some no matter what she did,
it didn't add up to the sum of what they expected.
Tried to give her mental medicine to say
she neglected people who are so precious.
As time goes on I hope they get the message:
Stand firm and hold on to His hand!
A mother's love never fails and it's always available.
When she's incapable of doing what she knows,
she turns to the "One" who's able to do it all!
She continues to wait for the release and to finally be at peace.

Writer's Block: 3rd Trip

As I dare to prepare for another trip around the block

instruments in hand, ready and cocked

at a slight 45 degree angle, thoughts dangle

here and there about things I'm aware of.

Paper awaits as my lyrical instrument makes its presence.

Hence, I then pause and ponder, mind starts to wonder....

"What am I gonna write about?"

In my mind thoughts pop up, then disappear,

I imagine walking 'round the block,

like Bruh Man wit' the slow bop,

taking each one carefully dissecting.

The Place

You touch my face gently
with your lips and hands and you command
to close my eyes so we may go to the place
that we go when we haven't seen each other in a while.
You put a smile on my face whenever I see yours or
when I think of all the special times we've spent together
when you kiss me my mind goes to a place
where it's just you and me in front of witnesses
but they don't matter,
all that matters is "The Place" you've taken me.
Sweet caresses, instant chills you give me
as you continue to kiss places on face.
I touch you as well...
your smooth, chocolate skin, kisses so decadent.
When I'm with you, I feel excellent.
You my love is heaven sent!
Time with you is well-spent
so when it's time to leave you
my heart feels dented.
I never wanna leave "the place" we go.
Will we come back? I really hope so!

The Dwelling Place

...And He showed me a pure river of water of life...
Revelation 22:1

He said to her, "Build me a temple where I can dwell"

I want a place where healing can take place and

Propel you to go to a higher level

I want a place where people can enjoy the freedom to worship freely

So that my Name can receive the Glory

I know each of you have a story

I know you've experienced pain and have a history

I want you to put ALL of this aside

And come where I abide

Come and lay it ALL at the alter

Lay here for a while and drink of this water from the river

Bask in my presence

Soak up all of the essence

I welcome you to let it go and let Me in

Let us dwell in love together

Here, in the dwelling place…

It's Between Me and You

There were a few instances in my life
when I've asked for people's opinion
and based my decision from there
but, life has taught me that at the end of the day,
it's between me and you, Father!

You will be there when no one else will.
You're my all: my friend, protector, provider,
the lover of my soul and even more!

At times, I steal away just to seek you
but then, I don't do it enough and I confess,
I need you more and more every measurement of time each day!
No matter how much I stray away, you're here.
It's my fault that we aren't as close as we should be and I'm sorry.
I'm seeking you more as I grow up
I can do nothing without you.
I love that what's been happening is between me and you
I love you!

You keep showing me what's good
and what's not so good for me!
You know how much I can bear
I'm forever grateful for You.
No one else can do what you've done and are doing for me.

It's between me and You

when no one understands my thoughts

and my mind or the way I handle certain things:

as long as it's between me and You,

nothing or no one else matters!

I love you, Father!

My Expressions of Me (1997)

(My first poem)

I feel as if I have no voice

I can't be heard

My thoughts are trapped within, trying to find a way out

I have no say in any discussion

I am cut off like a light when finished with use

I feel alone

All I can do is express my feelings to God

He hears all when nothing is being said

He knows my heart

I'd rather talk to myself so I could be heard

If I'm alone, at least someone or something

Could hear me, maybe a bird or the trees

Maybe I could get some response if the wind blows

Through it or I'm sitting on the beach

The gulls would cry out, which will let me know that I'm being heard

I feel so trapped inside, my thoughts inside are screaming to be heard

I feel used and my time is being abused

I get nothing in return but a broken heart or hurt feelings

Out of all this, I get headaches, banging, aching headaches

I feel like running away from home, school, associates, friends, church,

And my neighborhood

I am not happy, obviously

To smile is to let others know that I am alright, which is a front

At times I want to say things to hurt people but I don't

Instead, I let them hurt me and do nothing for revenge

Maybe that's the person I am

I can no longer take or go through this

At times I feel like being alone being my own person

Being an outcast is me, not caring about what people say or think of me

Everyone is wearing a mask of the same face; like front

Or trying to get with the "IN" crowd which isn't always good

I'd rather be on my own, worry-free, not depending on anyone,

I need to let things go, be free, be heard, be creative, be open and blunt

www.ingramcontent.com/pod-product-compliance
Lightning Source LLC
Chambersburg PA
CBHW071154090426
42736CB00012B/2324